WOVEN WORDS PUBLISHERS Presents

BREATHE

Deepali Gupta is a medical student from Mumbai who believes words have the power to heal, through their magic. She loves to look at the stars, talk to them, to meticulously observe the surroundings and the beauty it contains. Most of her work comes from it and her personal experiences.

She loves art and literature and keeps reading books all the time. At present, she is working with various publications as a book reviewer, and is involved in organizing poetry events. She also is working for various NGOs and performs slam poetry.

She has a poetry book called 'Emotions and Voids' available on Kindle. She has been published in various anthologies throughout the world by many publishers nationally and internationally. She has also been published by various online sites such as berlin-artparasite, magazines, e-zines, radio city and newspapers too. She is currently working on a short story, a self-help/poetry book.

Instagram: www.instagram.com/ofachesandhealing

Facebook: www.facebook.com/deepali.gupta.94

Email: dr.deepali_gupta@rediffmail.com

BREATHE

Deepali Gupta

Woven Words Publishers OPC Pvt. Ltd.
Registered Office:
Vill: Raipur, P.O: Raipur Paschimbar,
Dist: Purba Midnapore, Pin: 721401,
West Bengal, India.
www.wovenwordspublishers.net
Email: editor@wovenwordspublishers.net

First published by
Woven Words Publishers OPC Pvt. Ltd., 2017

Copyright© Deepali Gupta, 2017

ISBN-13: 978-81-934093-6-7
ISBN-10: 8193409361

POETRY

Price: $11

This book is a work of fiction. All names, characters, places, addresses and incidents are fictitious and product of the author's imagination. Any resemblance with any events, locales, persons-living or dead, is purely coincidental.

The author asserts the moral right to be identified as the author of this work.

All rights reserved. This book is sold to the condition that it shall not, by way of trade or otherwise, be lent, resold, hired out, or otherwise circulated without the publisher's prior consent in any form of binding or cover other than that in which it is published and without a similar condition, including this condition, being imposed on the subsequent purchaser.

Printed and bound in India

To all the times you have felt lost.

To the pain.

And to the healing.

To you,

With love.

TABLE OF CONTENTS

1- LOVE   11

2- BRUISES   53

3- HEALING PATIENTLY   109

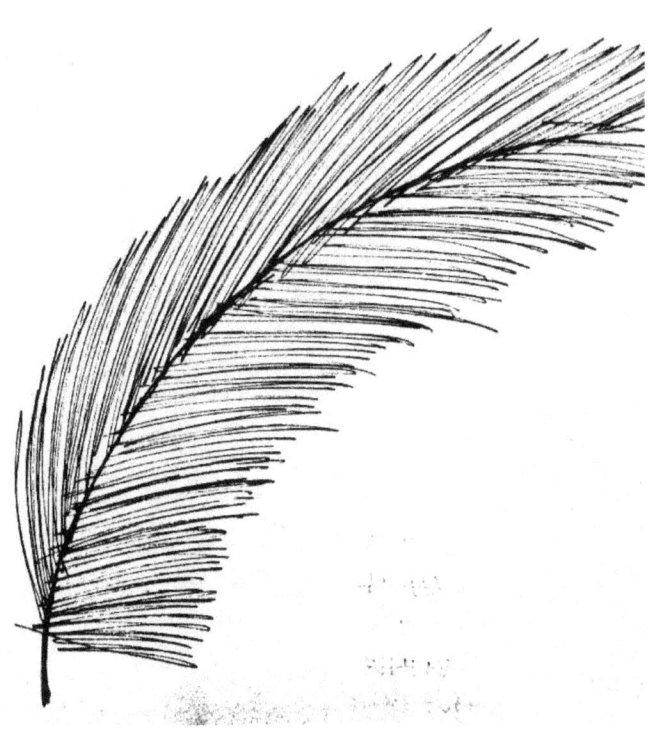

Love

BREATHE | Deepali Gupta

You hold me light as

The moon.

I am calm

And steady

In your arms.

Flawlessly beautiful.

Making me learn myself.

I am calmer now.

Like poetry to your skin,

~~I really think~~

I believe

I will never

Be out of love

For you.

- Yours.

BREATHE | Deepali Gupta

You speak

In a language

Only my eyes

Understand,

That stirs the Soul

And lips whisper.

- Sunk

You

Make me feel

A lot of things

Again.

The warmth,

The moon,

The emotions,

Little voids in me.

A little pain,

Anger,

And whole lot of

Love.

Fierce and consuming

Love.

- You make me feel

BREATHE | Deepali Gupta

There is sweet pain in life

And then there is

You.

- I need all of you.

Some days,

I feel

Mute,

With all of this

Inside me

Left unsaid

- Sometimes I speak with flowers and silence only.

BREATHE | Deepali Gupta

Let me in

And shed

Your sadness.

It is mine,

As much it is yours.

- I will make the moon out of it.

"You are mine forever,"

You say

Brushing my

Cheeks with your fingers.

I tremble wondering

If you really mean it.

- They leave.

BREATHE | Deepali Gupta

Peel your skin

I only see love.

- See through it now.

Your words are a warm blanket

Giving me

-The only peace I know

Sometimes

Distance,

And silence

Can be the only things

Love shares.

- Letting go

BREATHE | Deepali Gupta

Let it be tonight,

I already feel weak

To let you go.

And most of the days,

I wish to be okay,

But I do not promise

You about this.

- Be patient with me.

BREATHE | Deepali Gupta

Somewhere I hope, when we kissed

I had spilled myself between those

Sentences over your rhythmic

Breaths.

Maybe now I will always remind

You of honesty

And remembrance.

You look so honestly in love with me,

Today.

I call your name, but now only

Your existence resonates.

Will you

Walk beside me,

Just like the

Moon does?

- Walking forever.

You are mine,

You are a catalepsy.

- My sophrosyne

You need to

Learn

That

You can

Be your

own soul mate.

And you

Need only yourself to complete YOU.

- Learning

Watching you

Sleep peacefully

Is all I need,

To know

That I am all right.

- Days with you.

Your *Hello*,

Sounds a lot

Like

Undressing my

Skin, in pieces and bits.

- Vulnerabilities.

Your presence

Makes me guilty

Of all the sunsets

And sunrises,

I could have

Disintegrated into

- Merge.

To be one's silence,

To be one's poetry,

All over their

Mind,

Soul,

And heart

- That is what one wishes for.

Loving someone

Is cutting deep

Pulling out

Your heart.

Letting it only

Breathe enough

For them.

Loving is bleeding

 profusely, though you would

Not intend to.

Becoming

Another soul

With a thousand

Questions

And answers, to self.

Loving is never enough.

For love

Is all we

Bleed.

- Love.

You are

Kindness,

That still

Speaks through

Cruel times.

- Allure.

BREATHE | Deepali Gupta

You

Touch me

And I melt,

Losing my soul's

Battles

- What are you doing to me?

BREATHE | Deepali Gupta

The way

You look

Out

At the world,

The skylines

Or even the abyss,

Resembles

Van Gogh

Creating art.

- Altar of stars.

You are love.

Your skin

Is love

And cells are

Dripping honey.

You are love,

Even before

Anyone

Learned

To

Spill your name

Habitually.

- Don't let anyone mistreat you.

I'm

Away

From you

Yet intimate, And Close

In our memories.

I can never wash them away.

- We're still together.

Where was

Love when we started

Off,

And even when

We ended?

- Forced relations.

You are

The morning

Light,

I was searching

All this while.

    - Found.

Come,

Sit

Along

With

My loneliness

And me.

Tell me,

How does

It feels?

- Do you feel free too?

BREATHE | Deepali Gupta

My forehead

Touches

Yours.

My fingers

Entangles

In yours.

- I am praying.

BREATHE | Deepali Gupta

The night

Folds

Me

In all the ways,

You've left

Me.

- ...

You felt like embers glowing.

You felt like wind.

You felt like happiness.

You felt like so much more.

That I can never fathom into words.

BREATHE | Deepali Gupta

I like how you feel, warm

And melancholic.

I like how you feel

Like a winter morning.

BREATHE | Deepali Gupta

I never knew how to love and

What love felt like,

Until you made me speak

Each letter out

With correct pronunciation.

With time now

You are gone.

Now I wonder if that is what love is.

And how it tastes of unsaid goodbyes

Now.

BREATHE | Deepali Gupta

You were,

You are

You will

Be.

And always mean so much to me.

There were days when I started to

Feel your absence,

Just like your presence.

Bruises

I ate

The moon

Today,

With tears

In my hands.

- Disguise.

Be with someone

Who can calm

Your heart and

Soul.

- Only people you should be with.

How

Are we

Breathing?

With the distance

And soft anger.

- After you left.

BREATHE | Deepali Gupta

I am

Becoming

All the love

That you never

Gave me.

- Changes

I am all

The stars

And wilderness,

That breathes

Madness

Softly

    - Not yours.

BREATHE | Deepali Gupta

Learn

To love your aches.

For they

Are here

To stay,

To yearn

For yourself

In little breaths.

- It won't leave you so soon.

BREATHE | Deepali Gupta

Keeping safely

My emotions

To myself,

Or pouring out

My heart

to

Someone else.

- I don't know what hurts more.

BREATHE | Deepali Gupta

There is a reason

Why I don't let in your

Thick night,

Nor let you look into

Mine.

I don't want to be rehearsed easily.

Words would come flowing like

Rainto the clouds.

And melanin to sun.

I do not want that.

For there are

Like Oceans deep

My skin layers.

Peel it down one by one.

Slowly and steadily.

Learn and unlearn me over

And over again.

Take your time.

Go slow.

- Why I avoid eye- contact!

BREATHE | Deepali Gupta

Often people ask,

What is it to be an artist?

It is all the pain

That resides within.

Leaving in small seizures.

Stopping.

Crying.

Feeling.

In thousand ways, of vulnerabilities.

In reality and illusions,

Moon and sand,

Silence and chaos,

Everywhere and nowhere,

-In between everything.

BREATHE | Deepali Gupta

My soft mouth

Is cut into

Two spill of

Oceans.

- To speak or soak in silence.

And these

Eyes will carry storms

Very tenderly,

And you wouldn't know.

- Smiling.

Do not

Curse

Yourself,

Even for a

Second

When

They leave.

Because it

Was not

You.

It was the time.

It was the universe.

It is all that they could

Not be.

- Better

BREATHE | Deepali Gupta

Today

I called the

Number

Which used to be yours.

And

Somebody

Picked it

Up.

But I said nothing.

Even though there

Were noises

From the

Other side.

This

Is how it

Feels to

Stay

In your past

- Nothing good for you here.

I am

Feeding

And decorating

With soft scars,

All the

Places

You did

Not try to

Love me.

- Nightmares.

BREATHE | Deepali Gupta

There

Are rooms

Inside us,

Where we

Hide,

Learn,

Grow,

Heal,

Burn,

Bleed,

Wish,

Live,

Remember,

Let go,

Be,

Breathe,

Shed,

Rebuild.

- Blooming

My blood is of

Loneliness.

Frightened

By stories

That will break

Me down.

Verses to

My soul.

And here

I will be singing

Out my tragedies

Gracefully.

- Me, these days.

BREATHE | Deepali Gupta

I have become a moving desert,

A Living grey.

Warmth and I part ways

At times (I'm lying!)

I think and

I stand still.

For still

I have been,

Afraid of

Something

Always.

And even now.

It is the fear

Of the darkness

that resides

At the back

Of my mind.

- A dark place to be.

BREATHE | Deepali Gupta

I am stuck in this train,

Weeping

About regrets

And questioning

Life.

There are

Mountains that want to soften my skin.

There is the sun which wants to lick

My soul soft.

Salt and Water to cleanse my mind.

I have been dancing.

From here to there.

From here to there.

From here to there.

And everywhere.

There are roads

Which want to lead

Me to you,

And somewhere to your heart.

There is so much more

For me.

But here I am stuck in this

Train.

- Thoughts/depression.

BREATHE | Deepali Gupta

There is an ocean

churning inside me.

Raging blood.

Unexpressed

Thoughts.

It has and always

Has been

Swelling.

Soaking.

I am someone called I.

There is an ocean

Churning

Inside me

- Contemplating.

BREATHE | Deepali Gupta

A little gloomy,

A little found,

A little lost,

A little onism,

A little more,

A little close.

- How I feel today!

&&

Sometimes!!

__- I

->>,,,,,,

Cannot

   Spill

$4%%^ in

! language.

   - Communicate well.

It gets different

Each day.

I become wild

- Sonder.

Some names

Won't leave you,

And that is

How you

Will

Have voids

Formed within.

- Loss/lost.

BREATHE | Deepali Gupta

My body is

Full of battles.

You cannot

Come and

Leave brutally.

I am nights

That don't fit

On your tongue.

- Me.

Feel to survive.

Survive to feel

- Mantra.

It feels

Like I have known

These

Places,

Moments.

Nostalgia,

Now,

Then.

It is already written

And I am re-reading it.

Over and over again.

- Déjà vu

BREATHE | Deepali Gupta

Find me

Where the wild

Things grow

Inside

you.

Let me

Bloom

And

Let us

Stay.

- Quixotic

Here is

Your p(o)e(m),

Floating

And gathering.

- Give it a little more time darling.

Do not become

Simple for anyone

- Do not.

BREATHE | Deepali Gupta

Every tear

Is a verse

Of yourself,

Returning

In small breaths

- Glory.

Things that remain unnoticed by me-

1- I shiver when I speak, not letting you know how much you mean to me.

2- I am afraid to tell you so many things.

3- I fall for everything that cuts me through.

Something is in the pain that is growing and living inside me.

4- I am sinking into all the efforts I try to be.

5- I am hungry for things that make you feel alive.

6- I don't let anyone in, easily.

Emptiness

Teaches you

A lot about memories.

- You understand with time.

BREATHE | Deepali Gupta

Even silence is war;

The way we keep it

Below our tongues.

Hot iron.

Pain

In the corner of the eyelids

This is one

Of the reasons,

Why your eyes are so beautiful!

- Ask women.

How cruel it is

That you ask me to be!

And then blend me

Thousand times over.

- Changes.

I felt it.

I savored it.

At the tip of your tongue.

This soft taste of doom.

    -Kiss.

Dear sweetheart,

I know you are trying to push me away.

I know life has been unfair,

So, it is to me.

- Unafraid to love you.

The mold of sadness that sits

On my lap.

After happiness.

This is what breaks my heart.

- Every time.

How do souls get solitude?

What if there is so much

Light and healing in you?

But you're not letting it in!

- Mistakes

I am a distant memory to myself.

- Sometimes.

Sadness is not always put across,

Honestly.

- You need to seep.

I can give birth to life,

What could possibly be

More flawless, and beautiful

As this?

- Women

Why is everything such a gentle apocalypse?

- Today.

Love spreads like fire

And hurts like still water.

- Long time.

I am trying to make the world beautiful

And worthwhile again.

- When I close my eyes.

They say my words have matured.

No my aches have.

- Artist within.

I believe in stars.

I believe in distance

Between our dreams and reality.

The love we stay in and the one we avoid,

Pain perpetual.

In the heart and the situations.

- Truth we always hide.

BREATHE | Deepali Gupta

Healing

Repeat it

To yourself,

I will heal

Softly

And bravely.

- Again and again.

You are healing

By the voice

Of your scars.

    - You don't realize.

A weak song

Playing in the

Core of my bones.

Asking me to forgive

Myself.

For acceptance.

- Miracles

Relieving pain

Is to relive it

Gently.

Hold it up

And become

A new light.

Then let

It go.

- This is how it should be done.

Though

It will take

Time immensely,

But my heart

Will be serene again

BREATHE | Deepali Gupta

Love,

Whenever

You breathe.

In darkness,

You'll bleed light.

- Remember.

BREATHE | Deepali Gupta

You have to get away,

To meet yourself

In the middle of the way again.

- Sometimes.

You are the

Universe,

Full

Of gentleness

And love.

- Reminder

Live for yourself.

Respond to your emotions,

Feel them,

Have a lukewarm bath.

Rub some jasmine oil.

Nourish with more honesty

Towards yourself.

Love yourself

A little

More religiously.

- When it hurts.

Certain days

All we look

Is for

Conversations -

Deep, revoking

And calming.

- And look at the stars to heal.

Become water.

Flow.

The battles don't matter. .

- Becoming.

BREATHE | Deepali Gupta

Exhaustion is

Right only when

Itis for self.

Don't evacuate

Yourself, for others.

- Yourself

On days when you feel lost, underestimated and vulnerable.

On days when you take solace

On pillows of your soft heart and soul's tears.

On days when one song is playing repeatedly.

You're cracking under the weight of self and self-control,

Losing and loving.

You think you're just a cry baby but you're not.

You are a beautiful calamity, learning to carry yourself with all the resilience you have. -

BREATHE | Deepali Gupta

Put up during those days.

Spread them across.

Like a reel movie running in your head today.

Good days and bad.

Spill them into small clouds and make a wish to be softer, wiser.

Cut them swiftly from your eyes and keep them safe in the locker

Of your heart.

Pray for yourself, your body, make a pact to be more of you. Be wild. Make memories.

Live, read, breathe.

Don't let your heart break.

Let healing be your only routine.

Grow deep into yourself. Yearn for you.

There again is another year of battles to breathe.

- Another day to live.

Be there for those

Who are there for you.

Like dryness

To flowers when they wilt.

The melancholy that lives

In the sky forever,

Leaves marks on the soul

When they're willing to be hurt.

Be. Just be.

- Being there.

BREATHE | Deepali Gupta

There is a sunset in you,

Which will swell

When your heart

Is in your mouth.

- Calmed chaos.

BREATHE | Deepali Gupta

Learn to be

The roots

For yourself

- Firsts.

BREATHE | Deepali Gupta

You will

Keep bleeding

And also

Heal in the

Same process.

- Hurt

Morning comes

In slow

Motion.

And generously,

Only when

You are ready

To forgive

The previous day.

- Morning / bed sheets

BREATHE | Deepali Gupta

Grow In stars.

For the Ocean

Heals you,

While the Moon

Accompanies you.

How

magical

It is

To live

Below

Stars

With the scars!

- Human

I have been walking alone...

- This is how I heal.

I feel content being

alone today.

-Loving yourself.

BREATHE | Deepali Gupta

To know the difference,

    When to let go

    and when to hold on

    Eventually and lightly.

        -Questions I ask myself.

\- I am trying to write.

This. That. Everything

Close and slow pressed sunflowers.

So much is spilling inside me.

What do I spill?

-Writer's block

Find the lonely in me and recreate it.

- Find.

I'm breathing.

I'm leaving.

I'm returning.

- Fresh start.

BREATHE | Deepali Gupta

After being burnt,

You burn brighter,

You are healing.

Erase your grief.

Don't be afraid.

- Broken.

The way you gratify and celebrate

Others,

Do you do the same with yourself?

When was the last time you actually breathed?

And you let yourself go?

- Self-doubt and self-loathing.

-By the sun –

You

Are what they made you.

By the moon.-

You become what your soul is.

- Reality.

Silence is an art of

Self-worth and war.

It is in your mind, loud and clear.

Not twisting, not pressing your chest.

Let it flow like a river from the back of your throat,

From the back of your eyes,

Just write it down, simple and for once.

- Write.

Things to do when you set the moon to rest -

i- Don't become the night (for you are the moon)

ii- Cleanse your thoughts with boiling honey.

iii- See the wolves in you, don't get enraged.

iv- Bury up the memories in, just like dew.

v- Be soft and patient, for you're healing.

Be your own poem.

BREATHE | Deepali Gupta

Pluck in the gentleness

And rub it over.

Pluck in the guilt,

Pluck out the hate,

Pluck it and discard it off

Your skin.

Take all of it out.

Take only the warmth now.

Let it not grow inside you.

- Plucking and growing.

Forgive yourself, once in a while.

- Forgave.

BREATHE | Deepali Gupta

Your heart is warm,

Your heart is your only cure.

Keep it safe.

Wake up,

Spread your wings,

Now fly.

- Change.

To write is to meditate!

-What writing means to a writer.

Let's count stars,

Even if we are falling.

- Bliss.

Your wilderness shaketh the earth.

- You are so much more.

A note for you:

There will be days when your heart won't feel right and breathing will be heavier. But stay; you are important and mean so much.

Only time has answers, all humans can do is, hold on to this moment and make a memory of it. Do what amuses your soul. Experiment.

Experience. You've been wonderful and patient. Be gentle to yourself. Thank you for reading.

There are blank pages added to scribble out any words/thoughts that stir in your head. There are oceans in your wrists and head.

Use this book as a journal, return back. Read in small steps. make your own poems. Most importantly breathe. Keep blooming.

Scribble here

Scribble here

www.ingramcontent.com/pod-product-compliance
Lightning Source LLC
Chambersburg PA
CBHW031446040426
42444CB00007B/989